By Ryan H

© Copyright 2014

Python Programming

The ultimate crash course to learn Python Programming FAST!

TABLE OF CONTENTS

Chapter 1

Installation

When it comes to programming there are several high level languages available for the job. Although every programming language has a massive fan following, there is something special about Python. It is very easy to understand and follow that it has become the first choice for many developers.

In order to get a copy for your system, go to https://www.python.org/.

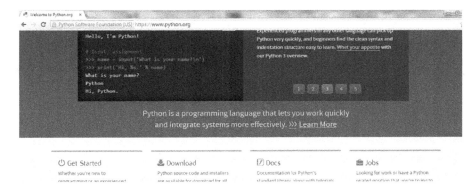

Go to download link:

Select the version right for your system.

Operating System	How to
Windows	When you execute the installer you will be presented with options, for most you will have to agree to default choices.
OS X	Double click the installer and follow the instructions. You have to just stick to default settings
Linux	If you are having linux operating systems then check if it has 'idle'. If yes, then your system already has Python installed.

Chapter 2

Variables and Types

Note: While learning about variables it is highly recommended that you try out all statements in the Python shell and see the results. You must also explore and experiment with the shell.

In any programming language variables are required to store values in memory locations. Variables are the most important aspect of any programming language including python. In simple words, variables are names given to memory locations. The values stored in these memory locations can be altered throughout the programming life cycle. Variables are stored in the main memory and are generally required to carry forward various processes and transactions. Since we are talking about memory allocated to variables it is quite obvious that once the variables are defined they will get associated with a physical address in the main memory. If we start accessing these values by physical addresses the code will get complicated so the addresses are associated with variable names.

In case of a static programming language a variable maybe defined as follows:
int variable_name =10;

It is not important to assign a value but it is important to provide the data type.
In case of Python it is important to provide value:
variable_name =10

The value '10' is stored in memory.

Now if we create one more variable as follows:
variable_name2 = variable_name

Then both the variables will refer to same object in the memory and new object will not be created. Another interesting thing about variables in Python is that if the type of value is changed then the type of the variable will also change. So, if the value of the variable is converted to String then the integer object created for it earlier will disappear and the variable_name will only fetch the string object.

Generally the approach in every static programming language such as Java, C++ etc. is that while declaring a variable you have to describe its type. Which means for every variable you have to define whether it is going to store an integer, or a string, or a float etc. however, things are different with python. Here, you need not define the variable type. Python will automatically detect the type. It is for his reason that Python is considered to be dynamic in nature.

The values are assigned to the variable using '=' sign. '=' sign here does not mean that the values on the right and left are equal, the expression given on the right is first evaluated and then the value is passed on to the variable. Therefore, unlike mathematics, Python associates the value or the expression on the right with the variable given on the left.

As mentioned above, Python is a smart language that has several built in functions that automatically detect different types of data and operate on them to produce results. So, after assigning a value to a variable you can easily detect its type with the help of function 'type'. The syntax for using this function is:

Type (parameters)

To print the outcome of this function writes:

Print type (parameters)

In order to assign a value to a variable the name of the variable is placed at the left of the operator ('=') and the value assigned is written on the right hand side.
You can also assign values to multiple variables in one go.

If you want to assign the same value to multiple values then it can be done as shown below:

There are several types of data types in Python. Python stores the information about the type of an object with the object. So, when an operation is to be performed on the object, Python evaluates the object rather than the operation to see if works on it or not. The most commonly used built-in data types are as follows:

1. Numbers
2. String
3. List
4. Tuple

Variable type	Description	Example
Numbers	<ul><li>int - integers</li><li>long- long integers</li><li>float – floating point</li><li>complex-complex</li></ul>	>>> val1=2 creates an integer object >>> val1=1.2 creates a float

String	Represents characters in quotation marks. Python allows both single as well as double quotes.	>>> val1='str'
		>>> str1='string'
		>>> str2="String"
		>>> str1
		output
		'string'
		>>> str2
		output
		'String'

List	Python allows you to hold a number of objects in an order in list. A List is like a container that can hold objects in a sequence and allows you to add or delete objects from the sequence.	Please refer chapter3
Tuple	Tuples are often used to store related data such as values of (latitude and longitude), (height and width),(age, name and sex) etc. It can be used to hold any number of data but once created the elements cannot be added or removed.	Please refer to section on Tuples on page number….

Numeric and String objects are immutable which means once created their values cannot be changed.

Variables are created on the basis of their values and not name. A value can exist in the memory only if it has a name associated with it. Assigning several names to same value means that you are creating several copies of the address of the same object

Tuples
'Tuple' is an immutable Python object which means that once it has been created it cannot be changed. Tuples are often used to store related data such as values of (latitude and longitude), (height and width),(age, name and sex) etc.

It can be used to hold any number of data but once created the elements cannot be added or removed.

A Tuple can be created as follows:
('a','b')
A variable can be assigned to a Tuple as follows:
tup1=('John','M',27)

```
>>> #Tuple is immutable it's value cannot be changed. The following statement wi
ll give a traceback error:
>>> tup1[1]='F'

Traceback (most recent call last):
  File "<pyshell#12>", line 1, in <module>
    tup1[1]='F'
TypeError: 'tuple' object does not support item assignment
```

```
>>> # Here is another interesing way of accessing values of a tuple:
>>> tup1[0:2]
('John', 'M')
>>> tup1[1:2]
('M',)
>>> tup1[0:1]
('John',)
>>> |
```

A tuple can be deleted as follows:
Del tuple_name
The following example will give you a better understanding:

```
Python 2.7.6 (default, Nov 10 2013, 19:24:18) [MSC v.1500 32 bit (Intel)] on win
32
Type "copyright", "credits" or "license()" for more information.
>>> #Create a tuple
>>> myTuple1=('Richard', 27, 'Male', 'Insurance and Banking')
>>> #Print it's value
>>> print myTuple1
('Richard', 27, 'Male', 'Insurance and Banking')
>>> #Delete the tuple
>>> del myTuple1
>>> #Try to print the values of the tuple now
>>> print myTuple1

Traceback (most recent call last):
  File "<pyshell#7>", line 1, in <module>
    print myTuple1
NameError: name 'myTuple1' is not defined
```

You can find the length of the Tuple in the following manner:

len(*tuple_value*)

```
>>> len(('a','b',9,12.75))
4
>>> myTuple1 =('a','b',9,12.75)
>>> len(myTuple1)
4
>>>
```

It is possible to Concatenate Tuples. Have a look at the example below:

```
>>> myTuple=(('a','b',9,12.75))
>>> myTuple=myTuple+('Richard', 27, 'Male', 'Insurance and Banking')
>>> myTuple
('a', 'b', 9, 12.75, 'Richard', 27, 'Male', 'Insurance and Banking')
```

You can also check if a particular value exists in a tuple

```
>>> myTuple
('a', 'b', 9, 12.75, 'Richard', 27, 'Male', 'Insurance and Banking')
>>> 16 in myTuple
False
>>> 'John' in myTuple
False
>>> 9 in myTuple
True
>>> 'Richard' in myTuple
True
```

The following is an example of how to carry out iterations in Tuples

```
>>> for x in myTuple: print x

a
b
9
12.75
Richard
27
Male
Insurance and Banking
```

Now let's see how repetitions can be caused in Tuples

```
>>> myTuple*4
('a', 'b', 9, 12.75, 'Richard', 27, 'Male', 'Insurance and Banking', 'a', 'b', 9
, 12.75, 'Richard', 27, 'Male', 'Insurance and Banking', 'a', 'b', 9, 12.75, 'Ri
chard', 27, 'Male', 'Insurance and Banking', 'a', 'b', 9, 12.75, 'Richard', 27,
'Male', 'Insurance and Banking')
>>> |
```

You also have the option of indexing and slicing in Tuples.
Consider the Tuple given below:

```
>>> tupList=('Hi','my','name','is','John')
>>> #The offset sarts at zero
>>> tupList[3]
'is'
>>> #you can have the negaive count from the right
>>> tupList[-1]
'John'
>>> #You can also fetch section from slicing
>>> tupList[:2]
('Hi', 'my')
>>> tupList[2:]
('name', 'is', 'John')
>>>
```

Chapter 3

Lists

Python allows you to hold a number of objects in an order in list. A List is like a container that can hold objects in a sequence and allows you to add or delete objects from the sequence.

Creating a list is a very simple. The expression is as follows:

myList = []

myList = [obj1,obj2,obj3,.....]

Python also provides support for computed lists. This is called "list comprehensions", which allows evaluation of expression a least once for each element in the sequence. The expression for list comprehension is as follows:

myList =[to_do for every item in the sequence]

Where to_do is the expression that is to be repeated for each element.

ACCSESSING LIST

-To know the number of items in a list:

Format:

Num=len(list_name)

EXAMPLE:

>>> myList
=['Sunday','Monday','Tuesday','Wednesday','Thursday','Friday','Saturday']

>>> len(myList)

Output: 7

-To know the value of the element at index 'i'

Format:

Element=list_name[i]

EXAMPLE:

>>> myList[2]

Output: "Tuesday'

-To know the values of elements between index 'i' and 'j'

Format:

Val=list_name[i:j]

EXAMPLE:

>>> myList[2:5]

Output:['Tuesday','Wednesday','Thursday´]

LOOPS

-To print items in a list:

Format:

For item in list_name:

print item

EXAMPLE:

>>> for element in myList:

print element

Output:Sunday,Monday,Tuesday,Wednesday,Thursday,Friday,Saturday

-To print both index and item in a list:

Format:

for index, element in enumerate(list_name):

print index, element

EXAMPLE:

>>> for index, element in enumerate(myList):

print index, element

Output:0Sunday;1Monday;2Tuesday;3Wednesday;4Thursday;5Friday;6 Saturday

-You can also use the buil in iter function

Format:

i=iter(list_name)

item = i.next()#this will fetch the first value

EXAMPLE:

>>> i=iter(myList)

>>> item=i.next()

>>> print item

Output: **Sunday**

MODIFYING LISTS

-To add a new element to the list

Format:

list_name.append(element)

EXAMPLE:

>>> myList.append('no day')

>>> print myList

Output:['Sunday','Monday','Tuesday','Wednesday','Thursday','Friday','Saturday','no day']

-To add items of another list

Format:

list_name.extend(list_name2)

EXAMPLE:

>>> myList
=['Sunday','Monday','Tuesday','Wednesday','Thursday','Friday','Saturday']

>>> myListMonth=
['January','February','March','April','May','June','July']

>>> myList.extend(myListMonth)

>>> myList

Output:['Sunday','Monday','Tuesday','Wednesday','Thursday','Friday','Saturday','January','February','March','April','May','June','July']

-To insert an element at a particular index

Format:

list_name.insert(index,element)

EXAMPLE:
>>> myList.insert(7,'now months')

>>> myList

Output:['Sunday','Monday','Tuesday','Wednesday','Thursday','Friday','Saturday','now-months','January','February','March','April','May', 'June', 'July']

-Remove an individual item

Format:

del list_name[index]

EXAMPLE:

>>> del myList[7]

>>> myList

Output:['Sunday','Monday','Tuesday','Wednesday','Thursday','Friday','Saturday','January','February','March','April','May','June','July']

-Remove sequence of items from list

Format:

del list_name[i:j]

EXAMPLE:

>>> del myList[7:9]

>>> myList

Output:['Sunday','Monday','Tuesday','Wednesday','T hursday','Friday','Saturday','March','April','May','Jun e','July']

-Remove an item and return it

Format:

item=list_name.pop() **#for removing last item**

*item=list_name.pop(index)***#for removing item at particular point**

EXAMPLE 1:

>>> item=myList.pop()

>>> item

Output: 'July'

>>> myList

Output:['Sunday','Monday','Tuesday','Wednesday','T hursday','Friday','Saturday','March','April','May','Jun e']

EXAMPLE 2:

>>> item=myList.pop(7)

>>> item

Output: 'March'

>>> myList

Output:['Sunday','Monday','Tuesday','Wednesday','Thursday','Friday','Saturday','April','May','June']

-Reverse the order of the list

Format:

myList.reverse()

EXAMPLE:

>>> myList.reverse()

>>> myList

Output:['June','May','April','Saturday','Friday','Thursday','Wednesday','Tuesday','Monday','Sunday']

Chapter 4

Basic Operators

In Python you will encounter following types of operators:
1.Arithmetic
2.Comparison/Relational
3.Assignment
4.Logical
5.Bitwise
6.Membership
7.Identity
The following chart explains all the operators in detail:

ARITHMETIC

-Addition

Format:

$a+b$

EXAMPLE:

>>> a=10

>>> b=20

>>> c=a+b

>>> c

Output: 30

-Subtraction

Format:

$a-b$

EXAMPLE:

>>> a=40

>>> b=10

>>> c=a-b

>>> c

Output: 30

-Multiplication

Format:

a*b

EXAMPLE:

>>> a=3

>>> b=10

>>> c=a*b

>>> c

Output: 30

-Division

Format:

a/b

EXAMPLE:

>>> a=300

>>> b=10

>>> c=a/b

>>> c

Output: 30

-Modulus

Format:

a%b

EXAMPLE:

>>> a=300

>>> b=10

>>> c=a%b

>>> c

Output: 0

-Exponent

Format:

**

EXAMPLE:

>>> a=2

>>> a**6

Output: 64

COMPARISON/RELATIONAL

-Returns true if two operands are equal

Format:

$a==b$ #if equal returns true

EXAMPLE:

>>> a=2

>>> b=2

>>> if (a==b):

print "Hello"

Output: Hello

-Returns true if two operands are not equal

Format:

$a!=b$ #if not equal returns true

EXAMPLE:

>>> a=2

>>> b=22

>>> if(a!=b):

print"Bye"

Output :Bye

-Another operator similar to !=

Format:

$a<>b$ #if not equal returns true

EXAMPLE:

>>> a=2

>>> b=22

>>> if(a<>b):

print "Bye"

Output: Bye

-Returns true is the variable on the left is greater than the variable on the right

Format:

$a>b$ # returns true is value of a is greater than b

EXAMPLE:

>>> a=2

>>> b=1

>>> if(a>b):

print "Hello"

Output: Hello

-Returns true is the variable on the left is lesser than the variable on the right

Format:

a<b # returns true is value of a is lesser than

EXAMPLE:

if(a<2):

print "Hello"

Output: Hello

-Returns true is the variable on the left is greater than or equal to the variable on the right

Format:

a>=b # returns true is value of a is greater than or equal to b

EXAMPLE:

>>> a= 22

>>> b=22

>>> if(a>=b):

print "Hello"

Output: Hello

-Returns true is the variable on the left is lesser than or equal to the variable on the right

Format:

$a<=b$ # **returns true is value of a is greater than or equal to b**

EXAMPLE:

>>> a=2

>>> b=2

>>> if(a<=b):

print "Hello"

Output: Hello

ASSIGNMENT

-The expression on the right hand side is evaluated and the value is assigned to the operand in the left

Format:

=

EXAMPLE:

>>> a=110

>>> b=20

>>> c=a+b

>>> c

Output: 130

-The value on the right is added to the operand on the left and then the result is assigned to the left operand

Format:

+=

EXAMPLE:

>>> a=5

>>> b=7

>>> a+=b

>>> a

Output: 12

-The value on the right is subtracted from the operand on the left and then the result is assigned to the left operand

Format:

-=

EXAMPLE:

>>> a=7

>>> b=5

>>> a-=b

>>> a

Output: 2

-The value on the right is multiplied to the operand on the left and then the result is assigned to the left operand

Format:

*=

EXAMPLE:

>>> a=7

>>> b=5

>>> a*=b

>>> a

Output: 35

LOGICAL

-Logical AND operator

Format:

And

EXAMPLE:

a=3

b=3

c=3

if(a==b and b==c):

print 'a=b=c'

Output: a=b=c

-Logical OR operator

Format:

Or

EXAMPLE:

a=3

b=5

c=3

if(a==c or b==c):

print 'either a or b is equal to c'

Output: either a or b is equal to c

-Logical NOT operator

Format:

Not

EXAMPLE:

b=5

c=3

if not(b==c):

print 'b is not equal to c'

Output: b is not equal to c

MEMBERSHIP

-Return true if the element is present in a sequence

Format:

In

EXAMPLE:

>>> if 1 in [1,2,3,4,5]:

print "yes it is there"

Output: *yes it is there*

-Return true if a variable is not present in the sequence

Format:

not in

EXAMPLE:

>>> if 1 not in [2,3,4,5,6,7,8]:

print "No it is not in here"

Output: *No it is not in here*

Chapter 5

String Formatting

Python uses "%" operator for formatting strings. A format for the string is defined and a tuple provides a set of values and then string formatting arguments are used to carry out the necessary operations. '%' is used with an argument specific which tells what type of operation is to be carried out. %s is the most commonly used directive.

```
>>> format = "%s is a student of this school and %s is in class %s"
>>> Michael = ("Michael","he","4")
>>> Mary = ("Mary","she","6")
>>> print (format % Michael)
Michael is a student of this school and he is in class 4
>>> print (format % Mary)
Mary is a student of this school and she is in class 6
```

Here is another way to use %s

```
>>> name = ['John','Michael','Chris']
>>> grade = [2,3,4]
>>> i=0
>>> while i<4:
        print "%s is in this school and he is in grade %s." % (name[i], grade[i])
        i += 1


John is in this school and he is in grade 2.
Michael is in this school and he is in grade 3.
Chris is in this school and he is in grade 4.
```

Now , let's have a look at some more format directives and their application:

-Formatting integer
Format:
%i

EXAMPLE:

>>> number='%i'%(4)

>>> number
Output: '4'

-Format decimal integer same
Format:

%d
EXAMPLE:

>>> number='%d'%(4.84)

>>> number
Output:'4'

-Hexadecimal integer
Format:
%x
EXAMPLE:

>>> hex_num='%x'%(16)
>>> hex_num
Output: '10'

-Float:
Format:
%f
EXAMPLE

>>> number='%f'%(4)

>>> number
Output: '4.000000'

The list doesn't end here. There are some more directives :
%c – ASCII characters
%e – float exponent
%u - unsigned integer
%o - octal integer

Chapter 6

Conditions

If you have knowledge of other programming languages then you would know the importance of conditional statements. Conditional statements are required to for taking decisions. Whenever we operate software, our choice of action decides the next step. A simple example is booking an air ticket. If you want o travel in economy class you will be presented a different package whereas if you opt for business class you will be given a different package. So, let's take a look at the conditional statements available in python.

-If statement along with else statement helps in taking decisions depending on the value of the expression. It works of the theory of true and false. If the output of the expression is true then the block of code for if statement will be and if the output is false then the block of code in else is executed.

Format:

if (expression):
code1
else:
code2

EXAMPLE:

a= 7

b=8
if(a>b):
    print 'I am greater than b'
else:
    print 'I am greater than a'

Output :I am greater than a

-To check multiple conditions and run the block of code for the condition that returns 'true'

Format:

if expression1:
code1
elif expression2:
code2
elif expression3:
code3
else:
code4

EXAMPLE
a=7
b=7
if(a>b):
   print 'I am greater than b'
elif (b>a):
   print 'I am greater than a'
elif (a==b):
   print 'Hey!! we both are equal'

Output: Hey!! we both are equal

A simple if statement can be used without any else or else if. Usage of simple if statement means that the lines of code should be executed only if the condition is true.

Format:

if condition :
execute the code

EXAMPLE

```
a=7
b=7
if(a>b):
    print  'I am greater than b'
print 'Good Bye'
```

<u>Output</u>: Good Bye

Chapter 7

Loops

Loops are required when there a need to execute a piece of code one or more times. As in case of all other languages, python too supports loops. Various types of loops can be defined as follows:

-While loop helps in repeating a block of code till a particular condition holds true.

Format:

while condition:
code_to_execute

EXAMPLE:
a=0
while a<10:
   print a
   a=a+1

Output: 0;1;2;3;4;5;6;7;8;9

-For loop uses a loop variable to repeat a block of code. Here are some points that you must keep in mind while working with for loop:

1.It must reference a list or range
2.For loop closes with a colon
3.The code that needs to be executed must be indented by one tab space

Format:

For condition:
Code_to_execute

EXAMPLE
a=['Sunday','Monday','Tuesday','Wednesday','Thursday','Friday','Saturday']
for item in a:
    print item

<u>Output</u>:Sunday;Monday;Tuesday;Wednesday;Thursday;Friday;Saturday

-Nested loops are used in scenario where there is a need to use one loop inside the other

Format

for condition1:
for condition2:
code_to_execute2
code_to_execute1

or

while condition1:
while condition2:
code_to_execute2
code_to_execute1

EXAMPLE

Nested for loop

```
i=['a','b','c']
j=['d','e','f']
k=['g','h','i']
l=[i,j,k]
m=1
for item in l:
print m
for element in item:
print element
m=m+1
```

Output:1;a;b;c;2;d;e;f;3;g;h;i

Nested While loop

```
x=1
y=10
z=20
while x<y:
```

```
print 'x= ',x
print 'x is less than y'
x=x+5
while y<z:
print 'y= ',y
print 'y is greater than x but less than z'
y=y+4
```

Output: x= 1; x is less than y; y= 10; y is greater than x but less than z; y= 14; y is greater than x but less than z; y= 18; y is greater than x but less than z; x= 6; x is less than y; x= 11; x is less than y; x= 16; x is less than y; x= 21; x is less than y

Normal execution of loops can be controlled with the help of control statements. The different types of **control statements** are described below:

-Terminates the loop execution and jumps to statement just after the loop

Format:

break

EXAMPLE:

```
x=1

while x<11:

if(x%2==0):

print 'x is even ',x

else:

print 'x is odd',x

x=x+1
```

if(x==5):break

print 'I will not go further'

Output: x is odd 1;x is even 2;x is odd 3;x is even 4;I will not go further

-Skips the execution of remaining statements of the loop and jumps to the loop's header line.

Format:

continue

EXAMPLE:
x = 10
while x:
    x=x-1
    if x%2!=0: continue
    print(x,'is even and less than 10')

Output: (8, 'is even and less than 10'); (6, 'is even and less than 10'); (4, 'is even and less than 10');(2, 'is even and less than 10');(0, 'is even and less than 10')

-When there is a need to have a statement that does nothing

Format

pass

Chapter 8

Functions

Function is a block of reusable code that is required to perform a set of actions. Functions help in organizing code. Python provides some basic user defined functions that are built in. Programmers can also build their own functions.

There are many built in functions in Python and it is not possible to describe all here. However, the following table explains some of the commonly used built in functions.

Function	Description
abs(x)	To get absolute value of number x.
all(iterable)	If all elements of the iterable are true then this function will return a true
any(iterable)	If any element of the iterable is true then this function will return true
basestring()	Used to check if an object us a string or a unicode
bin(x)	Convert integer to binary string
bool(x)	Converts a value to boolean – returns true or false
bytearray(obj)	If obj is callable it returns true else it returns false
chr(i)	For I in the range of 0 to 255 it returns a string of one character whose ASCII code is the integer i
cmp(x,y)	For objects x and y, the function returns negative integer if x<y, zero if x==0 and positive integer is x>y
complex([real[, imag]])	Converts string or a number into a complex number.

delattr(object, name)	This function helps in deleting an attribute of an object. The object should have a have a attribute with the name.
dict()	Creates object of dictionary class
divmod(a,b)	Where a and b are two non complex numbers, the function will return a pair of numbers that returns quotient and remainder.
file(name[, mode[, buffering]])	Constructor function for the file type
filter(func, iterable)	Construct a list from those elements of iterable for which function returns true
Float([x])	Converts x to number of floating point. If x is a string object then it must contain a decimal or a floating point number
frozenset([iterable])	Returns frozenset object
getattr (object, name)	Is same as object.name
hasattr (object, name)	If name is one of the attributes of the object then it returns true or else false is returned
id(object)	Return identity of the object
int(n)	Convert n to integer
len(s)	Returns length of object s
long(n)	Converts n to long
max(n)	Return largest item of string, tuple or list
min(n)	Return smallest item of string, tuple or list
pow(x,y)	Result is x raised to the power of y
round(j,k)	Floating point value of j is rounded to k digits

For defining your own functions you will have to remember the following:

1.A function is defined with the help of the keyword def

2.The function name must end with parentheses '()' followed by colon ':'

The syntax for defining a function is as follows:

def function_name(args):

    code_to_execute

functions are completely independent of the main program. You may consider it as a mini independent program that may require some parameters fr execution. The main program will only about the value returned by the function and it not concerned about what I actually did.

-Once a function has been designed it can be called from anywhere in the program

Format:

function_name(args)

EXAMPLE
```
def whoAmI(str):
   print 'I am',str
a='Apple'
b=7
c ='Cat'
whoAmI(a)
whoAmI(b)
whoAmI(c)
```

Output: I am Apple; I am 7; I am Cat

-Making a function return a value

Format:

def function_name():
code_ to execute
return value

EXAMPLE
```
def whoAmI(str):
   return str
a='Apple'
b='ball'
c ='Cat'
print whoAmI(a)
print whoAmI(b)
print whoAmI(c)
```

output:

Chapter 9

Classes and Objects

Object oriented programming languages make coding very simple which is why Python too provides support for classes and objects. In this chapter we will have a look at how object oriented coding can be done in Python.

For those who are new to the OOPs , the following information about the basics will be helpful.

A class is the basic building block for Python. It is created to define all the parameters that are required to create an instance of that class. A class makes use of instance variables, class variables and methods to define an object. It logically groups all the functions related to an entity. Technically a class can be created in any manner but while programming it is preferred to assign one class to one real world entity. For example for a banking software we will create customer class, employee class, loans class, salary class etc. so, that we can go ahead with programming in a systematic manner.

A class or an instance variable that holds data related to the class and its objects is called a data member. Variable defined inside a method of a class is called instance variable and a variable defined outside the methods of a class are called class variables. It is possible to derive one class from the other and the process is called inheritance. Functions defined within a class are also called methods.

A class is defined in the following manner:
class Class_name:
code(consisting of functions, variables etc)
The object of a class supports attribute reference and instantiation. In case of attribute reference the attributes can be referred in the following manner:
object_name. object_attribute.

Class instantiation on the other hand requires function notation. You will have to first create an instance:
object_name=class_name()
class_name() creates an instance of the class and it is assigned to local variable object_name

```
>>> class funcx:
        def f(self,x):
            self.x=x


>>> class funcx:
        def f(self,x):
            self.x=x
        def fSquare(self,x):
            self.x =x*x
        def pResult(self):
            print "the result is %s" %self.x


>>> firstobj=funcx()
>>> firstobj.f(7)
>>> firstobj.pResult()
the result is 7
>>> secondobj=funcx()
>>> secondobj.fSquare(3)
>>> secondobj.pResult()
the result is 9
>>> |
```

Now, you cannot move further without understanding the importance of 'self'. In python the first argument of every function in a class always refers to its current instance. 'self' is the new object that is created and whose function is called. The value of 'self' attribute is not passed explicitly to a function.

So, with information in mind let's analyze the code written above:
firstobj=funcx() # creates object of class funcx()
firstobj.f(7) #calls function f() in the class where x=7, self is current state of
#firstobj

A value of '7' is assigned to 'x' for firstobj

A python class may or may not have define a ___init___() function. Sometimes, when there is a need to create an object that are customized to an initial sate , the developer may define a ___init___() function in the class.

```
Python 2.7.6 (default, Nov 10 2013, 19:24:18) [MSC v.1500 32 bit (Intel)] on win
32
Type "copyright", "credits" or "license()" for more information.
>>> class Point:
        def __init__(self,loc1,loc2):
                self.x=loc1
                self.y=loc2

>>> location= Point(1,2)
>>> location.x, location.y
(1, 2)
```

Instance objects are created by calling the class name and passing the arguments that are required by its ___init___ function.
You can access the attributes of an object by using a dot operator and if you want to access a class variable then you will have to use a dot operator with the class name.

```
>>> class Point:
        pointCount=0
        def __init__(self,loc1,loc2):
                self.x=loc1
                self.y=loc2
                Point.pointCount+=1
        def displayPointCount(self):
                print "no. of points define are", Point.pointCount

>>> Point.pointCount
0
>>> location1= Point(1,2)
>>> location1.x, location1.y
(1, 2)
>>> location1.displayPointCount()
no. of points define are 1
>>> location2= Point(5,2)
>>> location2.x,location2.y
(5, 2)
>>> location2.displayPointCount()
no. of points define are 2
```

Common ways to access attributes are given below:

-Create an attribute for an object

Format:

objectname.attr = value

EXAMPLE:
>>> location1.distance=7.0
>>> location1.distance
Output: 7.0

-To check if an attribute exists or not

Format:

hasattr(obj,name)

EXAMPLE:
>>> hasattr(location1, 'distance')
Output: True

-Access an attribute of an object.

Format

getattr(obj, name[, default])

EXAMPLE:
>>> getattr(location1, 'distance')
Output: 7.0

-Set an attribute or create it if it does not exist

Format

setattr(obj,name,value)

EXAMPLE:
>>> setattr(location1, 'distance',10.1)
>>> getattr(location1, 'distance')
Output: 10.1

-__Delete an attribute__.

__Format:__

The delattr(obj, name)

EXAMPLE:
>>> delattr(location1, 'distance')
>>> getattr(location1, 'distance')
__Output: AttributeError: Point instance has no attribute 'distance'__

Chapter 10

Generators

Before going ahead with the concept of Generators it is important to get your fundamentals right about 'Iterables" and 'Iterators'. In other languages when we have to iterate over a list, we create a counter for the job. Have a look at the following example:

```
>>> days_of_the_week = ['Mon','Tue','Wed','Thu','Fri','Sat','Sun']
>>> i=0
>>> while i<len(days_of_the_week):
        day_list=days_of_the_week
        print day_list[i]
        i +=1


Mon
Tue
Wed
Thu
Fri
Sat
Sun .
```

Another way to accomplish this is by using range() as follows:

```
>>> days_of_the_week = ['Mon','Tue','Wed','Thu','Fri','Sat','Sun']
>>> for i in range(len(days_of_the_week)):
        day_list=days_of_the_week
        print days_of_the_week[i]


Mon
Tue
Wed
Thu
Fri
Sat
Sun
```

However the best way to do this in Python is as follows:

```
>>> days_of_the_week = ['Mon','Tue','Wed','Thu','Fri','Sat','Sun']
>>> for i in days_of_the_week:
        print i


Mon
Tue
Wed
Thu
Fri
Sat
Sun
```

Iteration over string can be carried out in the following manner::

```
>>> for alphabet in 'string_name':
        print alphabet


s
t
r
i
n
g
_
n
a
m
e
```

Iterations in file are also simple. Look at the following file object:

It is a text document. Now in order to read lines of this file through python we can implement the following code:

```
>>> f =open('football.txt')
>>> for line in f:
        print line


German World Cup winners welcomed home by hundreds of thousands

• Fans line the city's 'fan mile' for a glimpse of returning squad

• Joachim Löw's side hailed as national heroes after victory

• Pictures: the best images from Germany's victory parade
```

Iterables in Python are objects that can be iterated over. There are many other ways to carry out iterations.

You can use a list constructor to carry out iterations:

```
>>> list('Happy Birthday')
['H', 'a', 'p', 'p', 'y', ' ', 'B', 'i', 'r', 't', 'h', 'd', 'a', 'y']
>>>
```

Another way:

```
>>> list1=['a','b','c','d','e']
>>> get_ascii_for_char=[ord(x) for x in list1]
>>> get_ascii_for_char
[97, 98, 99, 100, 101]
...
```

The following example shows how sum() function can take iterables to produce a total sum:

```
>>> list1=['a','b','c','d','e']
>>> get_ascii_for_char=[ord(x) for x in list1]
>>> get_ascii_for_char
[97, 98, 99, 100, 101]
>>> sum(get_ascii_for_char)
495
```

The next example shows how iter() function can be used for iterations:

```
>>> list_for_iteration = iter(['a','b','c','d','e'])

>>> list_for_iteration.next()
'a'
>>> list_for_iteration.next()
'b'
>>> list_for_iteration.next()
'c'
>>> list_for_iteration.next()
'd'
>>> list_for_iteration.next()
'e'
```

With every next command, the next element is produced. When no more elements are left, it will display StopIteration as follows:

```
>>> list_for_iteration.next()

Traceback (most recent call last):
  File "<pyshell#21>", line 1, in <module>
    list_for_iteration.next()
StopIteration
```

Coming to Generators

In the above section you have seen various ways of carrying out iterations however these can be further simplified by the use of Generators. A generator object is an iterator. When a Python function is called, immediately the first line of the function is executed followed by the remaining lines of code till he point the function ends and the control is handed over to the caller.

We all have seen functions that return a single value at the end but what if we have a requirement for a function that must return more than one value or a series of value? In cases where a function is expected to yield a series of values it is important for it to save its work. Usage of 'yield'(as we will see in the coming examples) entails that the control is transferred temporarily and the function will reclaim it in the future.

In Python we make use of 'generators'(along with 'yield' keyword) to achieve this ask. Generators give programmers to easily generate code that has to generate series of values. With this there is no need to have a counter to keep a track of states between calls. Simple generators are often referred to as coroutines.

The main difference between a generator and an iterable is that the latter is capable of returning only one number at a time.

Now, let's take look at how generators simplify the work of iteration.

```
>>> def yrange(x):
        counter=0
        while counter<x:
                yield counter
                counter +=1


>>> gen_obj=yrange(5)
>>> gen_obj.next()
0
>>> gen_obj.next()
1
>>> gen_obj.next()
2
>>> gen_obj.next()
3
>>> gen_obj.next()
4
>>> gen_obj.next()

Traceback (most recent call last):
  File "<pyshell#21>", line 1, in <module>
    gen_obj.next()
StopIteration
```

When a call is made to the generator function it first returns a generator object. By this time not even the first line of the generator has been executed. The function starts executing when the next() method is called. The function is executed till it encounters 'yield' and returns the value that it has received at that point. To have a better idea about how this happens , we can put some print statements in the above example:

```
>>> def yrange(x):
        print "The function's first line has beeen executed now"
        counter=0
        while counter<x:
                print "Before yield my value is",counter
                yield counter
                print "Since next() has been called, I can execute the rest of the function"
                counter+=1

>>> gen_obj=yrange(5)
>>> gen_obj.next()
The function's first line has beeen executed now
Before yield my value is 0
0
>>> gen_obj.next()
Since next() has been called, I can execute the rest of the function
Before yield my value is 1
1
>>> gen_obj.next()
Since next() has been called, I can execute the rest of the function
Before yield my value is 2
2
>>> gen_obj.next()
Since next() has been called, I can execute the rest of the function
Before yield my value is 3
3
>>> gen_obj.next()
Since next() has been called, I can execute the rest of the function
Before yield my value is 4
4
>>> gen_obj.next()
Since next() has been called, I can execute the rest of the function

Traceback (most recent call last):
  File "<pyshell#46>", line 1, in <module>
    gen_obj.next()
StopIteration
```

So, generators are like special kind of iterator that can be used to generate a series of values. 'yield' in generator function is equivalent to 'return' in normal function. 'yield' helps in saving the 'state' of the generator function. The next value of the generator can be called by using 'next()' function.

Chapter 11

Regular Expressions

Regular expression in Python are required when there is a need to match or look for strings. Regular expression provides a special sequence of characters to do the job.

The regular expressions can be used with the help of 're' module. Whenever an occurs while compiling a regular expression the 're' module raises re.error exception.

The following methods are provided for sring:

1. Search- index, find and count
2. Replacing-replace
3. Parsing-split

Most search operations for strings requires looking for case-sensitive characters. When you have to conduct a case-insensitive search you must call string_name.lower() or string_name.upper() methods and ensure that the search strings have the right case to match.

So, let's get started with examples that will give you a good idea about how things work.

Example to replace a string:

```
>>> string_value='John is a good boy'
>>> string_value.replace('good','bad')
'John is a bad boy'
>>>
```

See how easily we converted John from good boy to bad boy. Now, here is another example:

```
>>> string_value='The house number 245 is my dreamhouse'
>>> string_value.replace('house','villa')
'The villa number 245 is my dreamvilla'
```

Now have a look at this

```
>>> s='motorway'
>>> s[:-3] + s[-3:].replace('way', 'side')
'motorside'
```

A very interesting example which says only to search and replace 'way' in the last three characters of the string and leave the rest of the string(s[:-3]). The following examples will help you understand the concept in more detail:

```
>>> s='motorway'
>>> s[:-3] + s[-3:].replace('way', 'side')
'motorside'
>>> s='motorway anyways which way'
>>> s[:-3] + s[-3:].replace('way', 'side')
'motorway anyways which side'
>>> s='anyways which way is motorway'
>>> s[:-3] + s[-3:].replace('way', 'side')
'anyways which way is motorside'
>>> s='anyways motorway is far away'
>>> s[:-3] + s[-3:].replace('way', 'side')
'anyways motorway is far aside'
...
```

Now, let's take a look at how we can actually use the 're' module

```
>>> string_value='The house number 245 is my dreamhouse'
>>> import re
>>> re.sub('house$','villa',string_value)
'The house number 245 is my dreamvilla'
>>> |
```

$ helps in replacing characters if they match the characters at the end of the string

```
>>> string_value='house number 245 is my dreamhouse'
>>> import re
>>> re.sub('^house','villa',string_value)
'villa number 245 is my dreamhouse'
```

'^' helps in replacing characters if they match the characters at the beginning of the string.
In the first example the sub function helps in identifying the 'house' at the end of string_value and replaces it and it ignores house at the beginning of the string. Same way in the second example 'house' in the beginning of the string is replaced and its occurrence at the end of the string is ignored.
When you want to mach a whole word and not a part of the word at the end of a string you can use \b as shown below:

```
>>> string_value='house number 245 is my dreamhouse'
>>> import re
>>> re.sub('\\bhouse$','villa',string_value)
'house number 245 is my dreamhouse'
>>> #since 'house' is not a whole word in the end of the sring in the above example, no changes were made.
>>> #now consider the next example
>>> string_value='house number 245 is my dream house'
>>> import re
>>> re.sub('\\bhouse$','villa',string_value)
'house number 245 is my dream villa'
>>> #since 'house' is a whole word occuring at the end of the string above it was replaced
```

You can also prefix letter r in front of the string if you want to work with raw string.

```
>>> string_value='The house number 245 is my dreamhouse'
>>> import re
>>> re.sub('house$','villa',string_value)
'The house number 245 is my dreamvilla'
>>> |
```

When you want to look for a whole word (and not part of a big word) in the entire string and then replace it. Then it can be done as follows:

```
>>> string_value='house number 245 is my dreamhouse'
>>> import re
>>> re.sub('^house','villa',string_value)
'villa number 245 is my dreamhouse'
```

Now let's take a look at re.match function which will match the object and return the result. Here, we make use of group(number) and group() function. While the latter returns all he matching subgroups, the former looks for a match at a specific subgroup number

```
>>> string_value='The house number 245 is a beautiful house and is my dreamhouse'
>>> import re
>>> match_object=re.match( r'(.*) is (.*?) .*', string_value, re.M|re.I)
>>> if match_object:
        print "match_object.group() : ", match_object.group()
        print "match_object.group(1) : ", match_object.group(1)
        print "match_object.group(2) : ", match_object.group(2)
```

Now let's try to understand the difference between match and search:

```
>>> import re
>>> string_value = 'house number 245 is a beautiful house and is my dreamhouse'
>>> match_object= re.match(r'beautiful',string_value,re.M|re.I)
>>> if match_object:
        print "match found"
        match_object.group()


>>>
>>> import re
>>> string_value = 'house number 245 is a beautiful house and is my dreamhouse'
>>> search_object= re.search(r'beautiful',string_value,re.M|re.I)
>>> if search_object:
        print "search successful!!"
        search_object.group()


search successful!!
'beautiful'
```

So, you can see that 'match' looks for a match at the beginning of the string whereas 'search' checks the entire string for match.

Chapter 12

Comprehension lists

Comprehension lists provides a great way to create lists and as you move ahead with the examples you will realize is importance.

In order to create a comprehension list you will use brackets that consists of a for clause and then it may or may not have more for or if clauses. Comprehension lists always returns a list.

Look at the following example:

```
>>> my_list=[1,2,45,3,2,65,287,2]
>>> my_second_list=[]
>>> for item in my_list:
        if item!=2:
                my_second_list.append(item)


>>> my_second_list
[1, 45, 3, 65, 287]
```

Now this is how it will look when you use comprehension list

```
>>> my_list=[1,2,45,3,2,65,287,2]
>>> my_second_list = [x for x in my_list if x!=2]
>>> my_second_list
[1, 45, 3, 65, 287]
```

So, in other words comprehension lists are more concise way of creating lists.

Comprehension lists can be applied on functions also. Consider the function square_root in the following example:

```
>>> def square_root(x):
        return x*x

>>> print square_root(2)
4
```

Now let's see how we can apply comprehension list to this function

```
>>> [square_root(x) for x in range(10)]
[0, 1, 4, 9, 16, 25, 36, 49, 64, 81]
```

Comprehension list can also be applied to files. In this example we apply comprehension list to football.txt file created in the chapter on Generators.

```
>>> football_file=open("football.txt","r")
>>> result=[i for i in football_file if "German" in i]
>>> result
['German World Cup winners welcomed home by hundreds of thousands\n', '\x95 Pict
ures: the best images from Germany\x92s victory parade']
```

So, do you have scenario where you would like to imply list comprehensions? It's about time that you give it a try.

Chapter 13

Functions of multiple arguments

In high level programming it is often required to define functions that ca take more than one argument.
The format for multiple arguments function is as follows:

```
def function_name(first_arg,second_arg,third_arg):
#use all the arguments to accomplish the task
```

If you have understood the basics of function then functions with multiple arguments should not be a problem for you. The following is an example of a function with multiple arguments.

```
Python 2.7.6 (default, Nov 10 2013, 19:24:18) [MSC v.1500 32 bit (Intel)] on win
32
Type "copyright", "credits" or "license()" for more information.
>>> def calculator(sign,first_number,second_number):
        if sign=="+":
                return first_number+second_number
        elif sign=="-":
                return first_number-second_number
        elif sign=="*":
                return first_number*second_number
        elif sign=="/":
                return first_number/second_number
        else:
                print "invalid sign"


>>> calculator("-",10,2)
8
>>> calculator("+",10,2)
12
>>> calculator("/",10,2)
5
>>> calculator("*",10,2)
20
>>> calculator("o",10,2)
invalid sign
```

Chapter 14

Exception Handling

While execution of a program any kind of error can occur. Exceptions help in handling errors in a convenient way so that your program does no crash. Exception handling should be used when you feel that you have a code that is capable of producing error.

You can also raise an exception in your code, this breaks the execution of the code and returns an exception.

Within Python you may encounter the following exception

Exception	Explanation
IOError	When the file does not open
ImportError	Module not found
ValueError	When a function receives a argument of right type but invalid value
KeyboardInterrupt	On pressing interrupt key: 'Del',"Ctrl+c"
EOFError	when one of the built-in functions hits an end-of-file condition (EOF) without reading any data

Exception handling blocks are created with the help of "try" and "except" keywords. The format is as follows:

try-except[exception_name]

The code that needs to be executed is placed in the 'try' block and in case an exception occurs the rest of the lines in the code will not be executed.

Try:

```
your_code
Except:
        code for handling exception
```

Look at the following example where first an attempt is made to divide a number by zero without exception handling. In the second attempt try-exception combination is used. See the results for yourself, rather try them out yourself.

```
>>> print "any number divided by zero is", 7/0
any number divided by zero is

Traceback (most recent call last):
  File "<pyshell#9>", line 1, in <module>
    print "any number divided by zero is", 7/0
ZeroDivisionError: integer division or modulo by zero
>>> try:
        print "any number divided by zero is...........", 7/0

except ZeroDivisionError:
        print "Not possible to divide any number by zero"


any number divided by zero is........... Not possible to divide any number by zero
```

With try-exception blocks you can also use 'finally' block and the code written here is executed whether an exception is raised or not. So, if we add finally to the above example the result will be as follows:

```
>>> try:
        print "any number divided by zero is...........", 7/0

except ZeroDivisionError:
        print "Not possible to divide any number by zero"
finally:
        print"I am glad this is over"


any number divided by zero is........... Not possible to divide any number by zero
I am glad this is over
```

Now look at the following example:

```
>>> students()
How many students are there in the class?
I think around: 30
oh you think there are 30  students in the class?
>>> students()
How many students are there in the class?
I think around: twenty

Traceback (most recent call last):
  File "<pyshell#6>", line 1, in <module>
    students()
  File "<pyshell#4>", line 3, in students
    number = int(raw_input("I think around: "))
ValueError: invalid literal for int() with base 10: 'twenty'
```

When you enter a number there is no issue but anything other than that will result in error. So, we can use try-except as shown below:

```
>>> def students():
        try:
                print "How many students are there in the class?"
                number = int(raw_input("I think around: "))
                print "oh you think there are", number," students in the class?"
        except ValueError:
                print " please only enter a numeral value"


>>> students()
How many students are there in the class?
I think around: 20
oh you think there are 20   students in the class?
>>> students()
How many students are there in the class?
I think around: twenty
 please only enter a numeral value
```

Remember that if you don' specify exception type in except block then it will catch all exceptions.

Chapter 15

Sets

Sets are used when there is a need to have lists with no duplicate entries. To understand how this works, try the following code:

```
>>> print set("the house number 245 is my dream house my dream is to own that house one day".split())
set(['own', 'that', 'house', 'is', 'number', 'one', '245', 'to', 'the', 'my', 'dream', 'day'])
```

The result is a set of unique words in the sentence.
Like sets in mathematics , sets helps in carrying out functions as intersection and difference which can be of great use.

```
>>> first_list_of_numbers=[1,2,3,4,5,6,7,8]
>>> second_list_of_numbers=[2,4,6,8,10]
>>> set1=set(first_list_of_numbers)
>>> set2=set(second_list_of_numbers)
>>> set1.intersection(set2)
set([8, 2, 4, 6])
>>> set2.difference(set1)
set([10])
>>> set2.symmetric_difference(set1)
set([1, 3, 5, 7, 10])
>>> set1.difference(set2)
set([1, 3, 5, 7])
```

Symmetric_difference provides those element that are present in either one of the sets so, *set1.symmetric_difference(set2)* is same as *set2.symmetric_difference(set1)*

Now let's have a look at the result for set1.union(set2)

```
>>> first_list_of_numbers=[1,2,3,4,5,6,7,8]
>>> second_list_of_numbers=[2,4,6,8,10]
>>> set1=set(first_list_of_numbers)
>>> set2=set(second_list_of_numbers)
>>> set1.union(set2)
set([1, 2, 3, 4, 5, 6, 7, 8, 10])
```

More elements can be added to a set as follows:

```
>>> set1.add(12)
>>> set1
set([1, 2, 3, 4, 5, 6, 7, 8, 12])
```

But a set cannot have duplicate entries so you cannot add the
same number again and again.

```
>>> set1.add(12)
>>> set1
set([1, 2, 3, 4, 5, 6, 7, 8, 12])
>>> set1.add(12)
>>> set1
set([1, 2, 3, 4, 5, 6, 7, 8, 12])
```

While add function allows you to add only one element at a
time, you can add more than one element with the help of
update function.

```
>>> set1.update([23,34,45,56,23])
>>> set1
set([1, 2, 3, 4, 5, 6, 7, 8, 12, 34, 45, 23, 56])
```

Let's now see the magic of copy() function

```
>>> set2=set1.copy()
>>> set2
set([1, 2, 3, 4, 5, 6, 7, 8, 12, 34, 45, 23, 56])
```

Chapter 16

Serialization

While working with Python you can use built-in JSON libraries as well. In Python version 2.5 the module that made this possible was called simplejson whereas in version 2.7 it is called json. In order to use this module it should be imported

```
import json
```

as follows

JSON data can be of two types:

1. String: this format is used to pass data into another program
2. Object datastructure: comprises of lists and dictionaries nested into each other. With the help of Python you can add, remove, list or search elements in the datastructure.

   Serialization is a process by which datastructure or a object state can be translated into a format that can be stored. The process of getting data from series of bytes is called deserialization. The json module helps in serializing to standard data format. Python also has pickle standard library that provides core serialization mechanism but the serialization format provided by it is not safe.

   'dump' method is used to encode data structure to JSON. It will take an object as an argument and returns a string. The load method is used to load JSON back to the data structure. This method takes String as an input and returns a object data structure.

```
Python 2.7.6 (default, Nov 10 2013, 19:24:18) [MSC v.1500 32 bit (Intel)] on win32
Type "copyright", "credits" or "license()" for more information.
>>> import json
>>> my_json_str = json.dumps(["sun","mon","tues","wed","thurs","fri","sat"])
>>> my_json_str
'["sun", "mon", "tues", "wed", "thurs", "fri", "sat"]'
>>> print json.loads(my_json_str)
[u'sun', u'mon', u'tues', u'wed', u'thurs', u'fri', u'sat']
```

Chapter 17

Partial functions

Partial functions in Python can be created with the help of functools library. Although Python s not a functional language but this library helps coders to wrie their code in functional style and one such feature of functools library is to create partial functions.
In order to use partial functions the following import is required:

```
from functools import partial
```

In partial function you can bind one constant value argument to a function and create a new functions that will take only the rest of the operations and amongst all calls the bound input will remain the same. To understand its application, have a look at the following example:

```
>>> from functools import partial
>>> #create a function for multiplication
>>> def func_multiply(x,y):
        return x*y

>>> func_multiply(3,4)
12
>>> #creation of partial function

>>> partial_multiply = partial(func_multiply,4)
>>> partial_multiply(4)
16
>>> partial_multiply(3)
12
```

Now , have a look a another example of how to find a cube of a number with the help of partial functions:

```
>>> from functools import partial
>>> def find_power(x, y):
        return x**y

>>> find_power(2, 3)
8
>>> find_power(3, 2)
9
>>> cube_value = partial(find_power, 3)
>>> cube_value(3)
27
>>> cube_value(2)
9
```

Chapter 18

Code introspection

Introspection is the greatest strength of Python. Code introspection is required for looking into other, modules, functions or object and retrieving information about them so that if there is a need for any kind of manipulation that can be carried out.

Built- in functions mentioned in the chapter on functions are used for code introspection. Have a look at the following examples.

Finding out type
```
>>> print type(10.4)
<type 'float'>
>>> from functools import partial
>>> type(partial)
<type 'type'>
```

Converting to string
```
>>> number=1
>>> type(number)
<type 'int'>
>>> str(number)
'1'
```

You can use the dir() function to know about the functions and attributes for an object

```
Python 2.7.6 (default, Nov 10 2013, 19:24:18) [MSC v.1500 32 bit (Intel)] <
Type "copyright", "credits" or "license()" for more information.
>>> number=1
>>> dir(number)
['__abs__', '__add__', '__and__', '__class__', '__cmp__', '__coerce__', '__
__getattribute__', '__getnewargs__', '__hash__', '__hex__', '__index__', '
, '__new__', '__nonzero__', '__oct__', '__or__', '__pos__', '__pow__', '__
_rfloordiv__', '__rlshift__', '__rmod__', '__rmul__', '__ror__', '__rpow__'
eof__', '__str__', '__sub__', '__subclasshook__', '__truediv__', '__trunc_
>>> str ='string'
>>> dir(str)
['__add__', '__class__', '__contains__', '__delattr__', '__doc__', '__eq__
', '__gt__', '__hash__', '__init__', '__le__', '__len__', '__lt__', '__mod
__rmul__', '__setattr__', '__sizeof__', '__str__', '__subclasshook__', '_fc
encode', 'endswith', 'expandtabs', 'find', 'format', 'index', 'isalnum', ':
strip', 'partition', 'replace', 'rfind', 'rindex', 'rjust', 'rpartition',
late', 'upper', 'zfill']
```

In the similar fashion you can use other functions that are given in table on in built function (refer to chapter on functions)

Conclusion

Now is your turn... become a professional programmer!

The course finished here.

You don´t have excuses now. You have the tools and you have the knowledge to board into action. So... turn on your computer, hot your fingers, launch Python Programming and start to programming NOW!

Thank you again for downloading this book. I would appreciate if you share your thoughts with other programmers. Remember that you can also post a review on Amazon, it'd be greatly appreciated for me!

To your codes success,

Ryan Hutt

www.ingramcontent.com/pod-product-compliance
Lightning Source LLC
Chambersburg PA
CBHW071029050326
40689CB00014B/3575